He Likes You Now What?

By: Annette O'Neal

Published by **To The Point Publishing**

Copyright © 2021 by Annette O'Neal

All rights reserved. This book or any portion thereof may not be reproduced or used in any manner whatsoever without the publisher's express written permission.

aoneal2058@yahoo.com

ISBN: 978-0-578-28279-4

Annette O’Neal

DEDICATION

To my mother, who taught me the value of Praise and Worship. Because in those moments, that is when God speaks, and it is always to lift someone else up and remind them how much He loves them and how important they are to Him.

I also dedicate this book to my dear friend and mentor, Dr. Reverend Tollisa Williams, who transitioned to Glory, February 18, 2022. She said write the book and here it is.

Annette O'Neal

Contents

Introduction

As a little girl around the 6th or 7th-grade, I remember thinking I wanted to get married when I was 25. I didn't know what kind of man I wanted to marry, but I did know I wanted two children, a boy, and a girl. And yes, believe it or not, my house would have a white picket fence. But, to me, this meant my life would be normal. Twenty-five would have been a perfect age, finished with college, have my own home, and driving my own car. So yeah, that would have been the perfect life.

Our family looked normal from the outside looking in. We had parents who both worked every day. My father was in the Air Force, and my mother was a housekeeper in the hotels of Las Vegas. I loved my parents and loved being at home. My most favorite memory was when we traveled to Okinawa, Japan. We were there for 18 months; my older brother and sister seemed to have a different life than my other three brothers and me. They were teenagers and got to go to parties and dances. While the rest of us played war games and watched Japanese TV, with shows like Godzilla and

Speed Racer. You know, the movies where the characters' mouths would move and later the words came out in English.

Okinawa is where my parents' relationship got just a little rocky, to say the least. My mother became a devout Christian filled with the Holy Spirit, and my dad became angry, desiring to have his old wife back. I can only explain it like this, from my perspective or as I can remember, the demons in my dad came out. He continued to go out and party alone, and she went to church. They became like oil and water.

You see, they both met in their hometown of Montgomery, Alabama. She was raised by her parents and grandmother, as her father was a railroad man, and her mother worked a lot as well. Her aunts and uncles were preachers, judges, and bishops. She had one sister, who was eleven years younger. Her parents owned their own home, which was left to my mother after her mom passed. Her father apparently passed before her mom. When and where I do not know of his whereabouts at that time.

My father was a twin, he had a sister, and they were both named Walter, Walter Lee, and she was Walter Mae. They also had a younger sister. His mother raised my father, while I don't ever remember hearing about dad's father. He came from the projects of Montgomery, Alabama. His mother sold alcohol and such out of her home. My grandmother was said to have been a very mean woman. She got angry with her daughter (my dads' twin) and cut her in the face with a knife. So, you see, their upbringing was very different.

My life did not turn out anything like I dreamed of as a preteen. Even now, at the age of 63, I have still not bought my first house, I do not drive a car, nor am I married. Not that I could not have those things, it is that my life took so many turns that caused me to become fearful. I allowed fear to settle in. It settled in because I welcomed it as my friend. It is what helped me keep away from doing things that would cause me to be disappointed.

When I was in the 4th grade, we moved into the house I grew up in. I believe this was the first time I went to a public school. All the other schools were on the Airbase. I was so shy in those days; I don't know what caused me to become that way. Years prior to that, it was thought I would become a lawyer because I was not afraid to ask questions. But, my shyness caused me to do something that my classmates never forgot. Maybe it was just the comfortability due to it being off the base.

You see, when I was in the 4th grade, I was so terrified of people looking at me I wouldn't even raise my hand in class. On my very first day of school, I had to go to the restroom so bad I could no longer hold it. I still could not muster up the courage to raise my hand. I had an accident right there on the floor. Not me as a kindergartner, no, me a 4th grader. I remember just looking forward as the teacher said, what is this? I never answered, and I did not move until everyone left the class.

I was such a smart little girl. Got good grades up to my 5th grade. Man, I could not get math for anything. I tried and tried. Back in those days, I did all my homework alone. Although I had both my parents, older brothers and a sister, I don't recall asking for or receiving help with my classes. I had very few friends at school, most of the girls shunned me, and I was too shy to ask why. I was trying to forget my last year. And I surely could not ask any of them for help. My only true friends were those I went to church with and my neighbor. She was a year older, but I never asked for help for some reason.

I would have been held back in the 5th grade if I didn't pass math. So, my teacher Mr. Homer helped me tirelessly to get a whopping "D." I was so glad that I passed. I will never forget him for the after-school assistance he provided. This was such a hard year for me. It was the first time I had a fight with a black girl, well, not really a fight; she hit me so hard I couldn't believe it. My nose hurt so bad it dazed me. I was called a "white girl," which baffled me because I am so dark-skinned. I think it was because I spoke proper English. I dressed differently because we were raised as Air Force brats. My mom probably picked out all my clothes until I was 14 years old. But, because she paid for them all, she still had to approve anything I wore until I was like 16.

When I was sick and got hungry I would carefully look down the hall and go into the kitchen and make a sandwich. I would eat the sandwich and run back to their room, which was in the back of the house. I was a very scary little girl. It carried over much too far into my adult life as well. I can laugh about that now.

My 5th-grade year was around the time I started exploring my mother's closet. I couldn't wait until I could fit her shoes. I just knew I would wear a size 8, just like her and my sister. They had the coolest shoes. And I always got a kick out of the shoe stretchers she used. I would forget to put them back from time to time, and she would tell me to stay out of her shoes. Then it happened. One day when I was going through her closet, I found my dad's clothing trunk he brought back with him from one of his Air Force assignments.

When I got hungry, I would carefully look down the hall, go into the kitchen, and make a sandwich. Then, I would eat the sandwich and run back to their room; you see, it was in the back of the house.

I thought and hoped it was clothes in the Trunk for the longest time, and he was moving out. Because, you see, he was an alcoholic and very mean when he came home. I almost said when he drank, but honestly, I cannot remember a day when he didn't. Not that he drank at home, but he was drunk every day. He was very mean not only to my mother but also to my brothers.

Did you know women can become addicted to pornography? I was exposed to something at a very young age no little child should experience. It became my best and worse friend. I spent hours with it instead of making real friends. It framed my way of thinking and interactions for years.

Pornography created an insatiable appetite in me for sex.

So, getting back to what was in the Trunk. The Trunk was full of pornography. These are some of the most explicit examples I have ever seen. You would think a little 5th grader would shy away from that stuff. However, I didn't. I was very intrigued by the stories and the men and women's great time in these (dirty) stories. The stories shaped my thinking on how I thought sex should be. It made it easy for me to be open to almost anything when I became of age. This is how I became addicted to pornography.

When my older sister moved out, I started withdrawing even more. Because now I shared my room with no one. Even though I was afraid to sleep in my room alone, I couldn't wait to be alone with those books is what I call them now. They so distorted my life and left me open for the enemy to teach me all kinds of dirty things. I shake my head now because he is so cunning as the Word says in the book of Genesis.

Late at night, when I thought everyone was asleep, I would pull those books out from under my bed and absorb as much of those dirty books as I could. I was so fascinated by the things they did. I knew I wasn't supposed to have those books, and normally if my parents told me to do something, I would do it. So therefore, when my brother caught me with them, he blackmailed me into doing things for him, and I did it because I was so afraid of what my parents might do to me messing with my dads' stuff.

As I grew into my teenage years, I became more withdrawn from reality. Before my freshman year, I started my menstruation (period) during the summer. That was when I realized I had to do things differently or get pregnant. You see, although I did not have real friends and every moment I spent out of my room, I was looking for a way to make my body feel good sexually. If some little boy liked me, then I would figure out how to get alone with him so he could touch me. I stopped letting boys touch me, but I did not stop touching myself. (WOW, this is a lot!) I knew I should not get pregnant because my mom had told me that I couldn't take care of a baby. So, I thought I should not have sex until I could get a job. Since at 14, I was too young to get a job, which meant I could not get pregnant.

I also started getting high that summer. I met a girl who became my best friend for the next year, and she introduced me to smoking marijuana. I enjoyed getting high so much because it took me away from the pressures at home and at school. Because of my new thing, I met many people and was involved in many circumstances that could have ended up badly. There were a lot of boys who didn't mind getting me high, but when it was time to pay up, I drew the line. They could touch me with my clothes on, but I was not about to have sex with any of them. I was waiting until I became an adult. That way, if I should happen to get pregnant, I would be old enough to get a job and take care of the child.

Man, boys would chase me, and I would run from them. They would pull my clothes down and tear my pants. I stuck to the fact that I was not going to get pregnant. Therefore, I was not having sex, no way!

I was headstrong and had high self-esteem until around the 4th grade. Then, I started noticing I looked different than the girls around me. And by my Freshman year in high school, I thought I was the darkest, ugliest girl in our neighborhood. I was very skinny. I later found out that although not everyone thought I was beautiful, I had no reason to think I was ugly. It was those times alone with the cunning one telling me how worthless I was. So, when I was about 16 and boys started talking to me and letting me know they liked me, I was an easy sell. All I needed was that one who was willing to spend time with me. I didn't need much, weed and cigarettes. I still did not want to get pregnant. Man, boys would chase me, and I would run from them. They would pull my clothes down and tear my pants. I stuck to the fact that I was not going to get pregnant.

Although I was involved in all these extracurricular activities, it was not with my parents' agreement. For my first two years of high school, I was in and out of the dean's office. I still got whippings from my mom and was grounded so much that my first two weeks of summer between my sophomore and junior year, I just sat at the edge of my front yard. At the same time, I watched my friends go to the park. That was our meeting place, the park where we had fun, told jokes, and got into a lot of trouble.

The park is where I met my first real boyfriend. I dated him for about a year. He and his mother and sister lived right on the corner where the park was. His sister and I were best of friends. He let his sister know he liked me. We were close until his sister turned on me and lied about something I supposedly said. She even went as far as to set up a fake conversation to prove I had been talking about him. He jumped on me. (That's what we called it when a boy or a husband beat his woman.) He gave me a black eye, and I still have the mark on my face to this day. I was not the type of person to accept that at first. I went a long time before I would even speak to him. Although we eventually started talking again, we were never as close again. And not because of me, but it was his choice. (I mean, why would I break up with him? After all, I thought, "He Liked Me.")

When we were finally done, I fell hard for another guy, he was so handsome, and he seemed to be really into me. I really thought he liked me. Even feeling that he liked me, I let someone else kiss me, which was the end of that story. I just didn't know how to set boundaries to keep myself from getting into trouble. I ended up hanging out with this guy and gave myself to him on my 18th birthday. Smoking all the time got me into places I never intended to go.

Even though smoking marijuana was a big part of my dysfunction as a young person, the main problem I had was falling for guys simply because they could touch me in a way that expressed "He Liked Me!" I have told you so much about myself for multiple reasons. The first is because it is so important to be comfortable with who you are before you get into relationships. Secondly, set boundaries. Don't just go with the flow. Realize what is important to you, and look for those things in others. The third thing is freedom. Make sure you are free and not bound by the cunning one and the things you have done in secret that bring you shame. If you are not free from sin, then what is in you is what you will draw. You may be looking for that special person, but if you don't know who you are, how will you know who he is? Until you have received freedom in

Christ, you will accept the fact that he likes you and seems to be into you.

You will get lost trying to please yourself through him. When someone simply likes you and does not honor the gift that you are, abuse is inevitable. I am not saying everyone will physically abuse you. Still, they cannot make you feel valued if you don't know your own value. What makes you feel good about yourself? This is an important question. And it is not one that I could have answered not even a few years ago. My answer and your answer should be the same. The fact that the creator of everything is my father means that my value cannot be bought.

Let me explain this because yes, I still like gifts and compliments. However, they cannot purchase me, and they can only demonstrate an appreciation for me. There is not enough money in the world that can make you feel good about yourself if you don't already. Sure, you can buy a lot with money, but broken hearts can't get mended, discouragement can't get restored, honor can't get revealed. Looking in the mirror and saying I like that person; is the only way you can feel valued by others. When you let others walk over you, it's because you somehow feel you deserve it.

So, when He says, "He Likes You!" you will need to find out what else he has to offer. Good times are great if you are not planning on having a life together. But if you live a purposeful life in Christ Jesus, you will need to know more about him than he makes me smile. God should be the first one you talk to about him.

Chapter 1 The Trunk

"Meats for the belly, and the belly for meats: but God shall destroy both it and them. Now the body is not for fornication, but for the Lord; and the Lord for the body."

1 Cor. 6:13 NKJ

The Trunk represents an open door, the foothold the Holy Spirit speaks about through the Apostle Paul in the book of Ephesians, chapter 4. Although I was a young child, I knew better than to go into my fathers' things. Disobedience at any age brings consequences. My act of disobedience allowed me to be drugged through the mud by satan. Even when I thought I was in control of my life, he was. He was orchestrating how I used my body. I was open to being shamed by him. I used men, and they used me. For what, the excitement that soon ended just as quickly as it started. I call sex 30 seconds of pleasure. Because when it's done, it's done.

It can be the greatest feeling and have the best outcome when it is done for love. God gave us this wonderful gift to be used to express our highest level of love to our spouses. He gave it to us to enjoy while we fulfill his command to be fruitful and multiply. But, unfortunately, we have mistaken it for love. We have made it complicated. We have destroyed our society because of it. Now, we use drugs and alcohol to try and compensate for the loss of satisfaction that making love once brought.

You see, the father, our creator, has given us the whole earth to enjoy. When He created Adam and Eve and the animals, he made us love each other. He created Man and Woman to care for each other, to lift each other up. His intent was never for us to tear each other down. Yet, we do it and tear each other down when we use each other for sex. Intimacy between a man and woman was meant to join them together as one. Men and women exchange truths about each other during this time of closeness; Words cannot accurately describe what you feel for each other. Sharing your most valued possession for a few moments of pleasure is belittling yourself. Would you sell a precious stone for a few seconds of happiness? Well, that is what happens when you fornicate.

The Bible tells us that "Now the body is not for fornication; it is for the Lord." (1Corinthians 6:13)

Although sexual immorality is not the only thing that the Trunk represented, it was an open door. Now, because my father brought that Trunk (dirty books), he opened the door to the enemy to run rampant in his home. I was not the only one looking at those books, so was my brother. That's how he knew what I was doing. Those details shaped his way of thinking as it did for me. Although he married at an early age, he initially had some backward thinking about marriage. Thank God the Lord could correct him on some of those things.

The Trunk is what led me to my life of "stinking thinking," as some call it. What does the Trunk represent for you? How was the devil able to get a foothold on you? Was it the first time you stole from someone, was it a lie you told, was it the first cigarette you smoked, or the first drink you had? God can heal you from all the repercussions, whatever the disobedient act was. He is a loving and forgiving God. You just have to ask Him to help you.

We as parents must be aware of everything we bring into our homes. We are responsible for a lot of things our children experience. It is called the iniquities of the forefathers. You see, just by looking into the pandora's box that was the Trunk, my whole way of thinking was shaped by the cunning one. Later, my mom told me that she asked my dad to get rid of those books. Has those books allowed me to be open to prostitution as if my body was worthless. Because of the things I heard and saw, I was easily persuaded to sell myself for pennies. The Bible says that if I had maintained my position of virtue, I would have been considered more valuable than rubies.

What is in the Trunk of your mind that God needs to replace? There is only one way to change, and that is through God's Word. You must have a desire to do things God's way. Fornication is a trick from the enemy. Society had changed so much since the 70's when we became a free for all type of culture. We as a people have shunned the laws of the Lord and have not kept ourselves clean for His use. So, now our children are suffering because they are so unhappy. They cannot be happy serving two masters, God and Mammon (self). Mammon represents money, which can be described as selfishness, which can be construed as an idol.

Lets' Pray

In the name of Jesus, Father God reveal to us our idols. Show us, Lord, what we need to do so that we can walk worthy of the calling you have for us. Forgive us for making our bodies unholy by using them differently than what you created them for.

Lord, we know that you forgive us for all things. We thank you for wiping our slates clean. We ask that you do not hold our sins against our children. We break every bloodline curse that we created In the name of Jesus. We thank you for your blessing as it is to a thousand generations. We thank you for the blood of Jesus that cleanses us from all unrighteousness.

Read Isaiah 53 in this chapter; it tells you all that Jesus did for us on the cross.

Chapter 2 Let's Work on You

Although I was raised in the church from such a young age, it is part of my youngest memories. I still did not come to the Lord until I was about 38 years old. I had so much junk in me, and of course, it multiplied by leaps and bounds with all the crazy relationships I had. Just because I am heterosexual doesn't mean all my relational problems stemmed from the ones I had with men. My problems stemmed from the relationship I had with myself. My thoughts of insecurities. My lack of self-worth. And most of all, what were my true boundaries?

Although I am still working on some things and will probably for the rest of my life, I am secure in who God created me to be. I am a mother, a daughter, a grandmother, and a very loyal friend. Those are things you can take to the bank about me. But, I am also called of God to teach His Word. To make it plain and simple, to let everyone know that there is no fulfillment without Christ Jesus. Because He came to set us free.

One day when Jesus was teaching in the synagogue, he grabbed for the scroll from Isaiah 61:1 as recorded in Luke 4:18.

"The Spirit of the Lord is upon me, for He has anointed me to bring Good News to the poor, He has sent me to proclaim that captives will be released, That the blind will see, that the oppressed will be set free. (Luke 4:18 NLT)

So, we can be set free from whatever holds us, hostage through our belief in Christ. These things that hold us hostage are what we have come to accept as a part of who we are. Nothing that is against Gods' law is true. So, anything that happened in our childhood past that causes us to act out or feel a certain way about who we are is a lie. The only truth is what God says about you. The things that you experience are real. However, they have no real right to dictate how you should function. Why, because Jesus Christ set you free.

Some years ago, a young friend asked me what the big deal about Jesus was dying on the cross. She did not mean it wasn't a big deal; what she meant was what did it do for me. She said she did not understand how his life being sacrificed changed anything for her. I tried explaining to her that because Jesus died for us, we no longer have to pay for our sins. We are no longer required to sacrifice animals, and Jesus was our sacrifice. He did it. By him sacrificing himself, he paid for our sins. Something miraculous happens when we start seeking answers about Jesus. As she began to ask questions, Holy Spirit started to reveal the fullness of who we are in Christ Jesus to her. She was only in my life for about a year, and during this time, her life seemed chaotic. Still, as she started seeking God more and going back to church more often, her chaotic life settled down. She got promoted at her job, and her whole attitude about life changed.

You see, the only way you can understand the magnitude of what Jesus did for us is by the Holy Spirit. The Holy Spirit reveals all truth. Most of us believe that Jesus Christ died on the cross and was raised from the dead by God. But most of us don't understand that what this means is that we are no longer slaves to sin. We do not have to bow down to our lustful desires. That God created us to be worshippers of Him and Him only. When we worship Him with our whole heart, He changes us into children of freedom. It's true, and we will no longer have a sincere desire to do anything that does not please the father. Let me reiterate we will no longer have a sincere desire.

What I mean is as simple as this, our spirit is willing to do things Gods' way, but our bodies exist in this world, and sometimes it will call out for things that are not Godly. Our body is not who we were created to be. Our body is an outer shell that allows us to participate in the earth's realm. It enjoys doing fleshly things, eating, drinking, and being merry. But, it also enjoys doing those things that are not good for you. Like me, for instance, my body sometimes cries out for my past desires, but as a true worshipper of God in my spirit, it does not bring me happiness, nor does it bring me satisfaction. Instead, it makes me want more of God because when you come to Him fully, nothing else will satisfy you.

So, freedom, what does that mean to you? What things have you bound? What are the lustful thoughts that hold you hostage? You might not even realize that you are hostage. Here is one way you can tell. When you are finished fulfilling the desires of the flesh, does it completely fulfill you, or is it temporary? You see, you feel complete when you give your everything to God. You feel that nothing is missing. He fills every void.

You might say, then why do I need to be in a relationship with others? The answer to that is that God created us to work together. We can't have children alone; we can't complete any assignments He gives us alone. God desires that we help each other. He created man and woman so that man did not have to be alone. (see Gen 2:18)

I was such a mess that I really thought that I had to have multiple men in my life to satisfy me. Pornography created an insatiable appetite in me for sex. So much so that pornography alone no longer would satisfy me. So I started going out with all these different men with all their different personalities. Oh my! And then I took on all these personalities. I became someone I no longer recognized. Honestly, I couldn't relate to these men, and something was lacking in each one of them. That something was God. These men were not the problem, I was. I was unfulfilled, and I was afraid of everything. I was dissatisfied with everything, and I was angry with everybody. I needed peace.

One Wednesday morning, I cried out to the Lord and gave my life to Him. Little by little, through the Holy Spirit, He began to change me. He first gave me a desire to want to know Him. As I began to know my Lord, so many things changed about me so quickly. It's not like I fit in with the crowd I ran with anyway, but it became more apparent, and the separation from them happened quickly. Before I knew it, I was part of a completely different group of people in less than two years. I was not even invited to the events where I would have been normally invited.

As the Lord separated me, he took me through the best training ever. It was called Freedom in Christ. I learned so much about God's love and his faithfulness towards me.

If you desire to be free from the sins that so easily bind you, I will lead you in prayer. The next thing I suggest is finding a good bible teaching church. Not just a Sunday morning Wednesday night church, no find a church that will go deeper. A church that holds sessions that teach about Freedom in Christ.

Let's Pray:

Father in the Name of Jesus, I ask that you lead and guide me into all truth by your Holy Spirit. Teach me your ways. Open my eyes that I might see the error of my ways. Lord, I ask that you forgive me for all my sins. Jesus, thank you for dying on the cross so that I can be free.

Father, lead me to the church you want me to attend so that I can learn more about you.

Thank you for your love towards me.

Amen

Chapter 3 Let's Work on Trust

Without trust, it is impossible to develop any type of friendship. I had been so mistreated by people I couldn't trust anyone. I was so afraid to let my guard down. I had friends misuse me, but they also misused my children in the worst way. I had men lie to me, and I had female friends betray me. I had friends lie about me, and they broadcast everything they did to help me. I had people turn their backs on me. Even those who knew I did them no wrong treated me as if I had.

I am not saying I was a good person, I am loyal to my friends, but outside of that, I had no actual boundaries for dating men, any man that "Liked Me," and I liked them. I did not date married men unless he was separated from his wife. They could not be dating or living with someone I considered a friend. But everyone else I had an eye for had an opportunity to be with me. And I don't mean to have a relationship; I meant he could possibly lay with me. After all, I wasn't looking for marriage, nor was I looking for a roommate.

I have never been one to give up on my friendships easily. People have to initiate a breaking away with me. If they stop communicating with me or tell me they do not want to be friends anymore; I will stop reaching out to you. Once I am your friend, I am always your friend. We may deal with each other from a distance, but I will love you forever. I have very few people I have called friends, except those who are my childhood friends. We have a different type of bond. Our experiences bind us together forever.

I am talking about people who you chose to associate with as adults. Those you thought would be there no matter what. I mean, you can probably count on one hand those people. Well, I certainly can. I had one friend whom I loved like she was my sister. We did almost everything together. She knew more about me than the men I dated. She betrayed me. I don't hold it against her because it is her right to choose to live her life any way she feels. I tried so hard to hold on to that friendship that I ended up hurting my family even more.

My oldest daughter would say things like, "if she were really your friend, she wouldn't have done that." After that, she became very bitter about the things my friends did to us. Unforgiveness is a danger zone. It causes bitterness and anger.

The betrayal, of course, had to do with a man. As a matter of fact, a portal of betrayal opened. Not only did she betray me, but three other men during this same season of my life betrayed me as well. I saw that I could not trust any man around my daughters. So I decided that I would not date.

Shortly after, I was introduced to the Holy Spirit. He helped me in so many ways. I thought I was fully delivered from the fear that caused distrust. Until one Sunday, my pastor teaching on Marriage and Family did a demonstration. He introduced the congregation to several couples who had successfully blended together as a family. I will never forget that moment I realized I distrusted men so much that I would never be able to bring a man into my home. I would never trust a man around my children again. Even if God himself was showing me, I could trust Him to protect me. I wept uncontrollably. Even now, it's a scary thing, but I trust that if God brings a man into my life, He will protect us. The thing is to know it is God, or the same cycles could easily occur. God will not bring you a man into your life just to bring you pleasure. No, it will be Gods' good pleasure to give you good gifts. So, it would be for Gods' purpose. Do you know that

He has plans for you that will cause you to be prosperous in every aspect of your life?

Psalms 91:2 I will say to the LORD, He is My refuge and my fortress, my God, in whom I trust." (KJV)

Proverbs 3:5-6 "Trust in the LORD with all your heart And lean not on your own understanding; In all your ways acknowledge Him, And He shall direct your paths." (NKJV)

That Sunday, the Lord set me free. He allowed me to see that I was not operating from a place of choice. I was still operating in fear. When I realized thoughts of betrayal were still tormenting me, and I was still harboring fear, I released all my emotions to God. It is hard to let go when something so real has a gripping control over you. Where I thought I was choosing to stay single, I was actually just running from the possibility of being betrayed again. Once the Lord revealed it to me, it was then up to me to accept His deliverance plan. So, I opened my heart to the possibility of having a relationship with a man.

One of my old friends came around, and I just knew he was sent from God. He may have been sent for a different reason because he told me he wanted to get married under no circumstances. I was not what he was looking for in marriage. I was devastated. However, it was not his fault, and I should have asked God who he was to be in my life. He was not a Christian man; he didn't even attend church. I am still open to whatever God has for me. I have to honestly admit that I enjoy being alone at this time in my life. But not my will be done but Gods. I know many of you say God does not make us marry. No, He doesn't; however, He knows what we need to fulfill His purpose here on the earth.

I also learned through that last ordeal of allowing someone to become intimately close to me without confirming with God. I had fallen back into trusting my five senses and not relying on God to guide me, he did say he would direct my paths. Which means ask Him who is this person in my life, and is he from you? So I have to stop trusting in my own senses and trust God. Even if, "He does like me." Nonetheless, that is not enough! I will no longer settle for anything less than what God says is acceptable.

Did you know Holy Spirit reveals the truth to us? I remember a friend prophesied to me that a man would come into my life for my daughter. Not for me. And now that I can look at the relationship, he may have been sent to help my youngest daughter. She needed a father, which is precisely what God told me that Sunday morning; That he needed me to be open to receive the man he sends for my daughter.

My youngest daughter's father died when she was 8, and she has missed him ever since. Even though we did not live in the same state, I moved before she turned 1. She spent time with him and loved him very much.

In the Bible, Paul, the Apostle said, *that if we can abstain from sexual relations, that is good. However, if you cannot, then it is best to marry. For It is better to marry and not to burn.* (1Corinthians 7 KSV) You see, for those of us who are children of God, we cannot have sexual relations and live with others that we are not married to. We are children of the Kingdom of God, and He forbids it. Well, He won't stop us, but we will not live according to what He desires for us. The Bible tells us in Revelation 22, "those who will inherit the Kingdom of Heaven and those that live in sin will not."

Therefore, if we want to live our lives according to the blessing of God, we must do things His way. If we do things His way, we can trust that God will provide for and protect us. He will not leave our necessities to another person to take care of us. Now, God will allow someone to be a blessing to you because He established the earth that way. God set it up so that if we sow, we will reap. The Bible says that if you are friendly, then you will have friends.

Proverbs 18:24 A man that hath friends must shew **himself friendly***: and there is a friend that sticketh closer than a brother.*

It is not easy to trust after you have been abused or mistreated but know that God has good people waiting for you. He wants you to enjoy life. And remember, in Genesis, "God said it is not good for us to be alone. So he created women to be the helpmeet (helper) to the man." There is only one way you can be one hundred percent made whole, and that is by relying on God, through Holy Spirit, to heal you. And heal you, He will.

I can honestly say I have some of the best people in my life now that I can call friends. God placed them there. They are people I can trust with my family. My friends love me because God has given me to them as a friend. My friends trust me, and I trust them. I can rely on them for almost anything. I say almost because my friends are people who listen to the voice of God, and if He tells them not to do something for me and they have it in their ability to do it, they will not. Why? Because they know God has my best interest in mind, and He will provide. Godly friends are those that hear from God on your behalf. They trust God. Therefore, they are trustworthy.

It's so funny; today, I sit on my bed writing while healing from Covid-19. My chest hurts, my head hurts, and I can't smell anything. But, with everything in me, I give God Praise because I know God has me without a shadow of a doubt. He has me in the palm of His hand. I know that God is always there for me.

So, if you are ready to let go and let God, repeat this prayer:

Heavenly Father in the name of Jesus! Your Word says, "Many are the afflictions of the righteous, but you have delivered us out of them all." (Psalm 34:19 KJV) God you also told us, Jesus, that in this world, we will have trouble, but that we can be of good cheer because you have already overcome this world. (John 16:33) Lord, thank you for saving us. Thank you, Lord, that no matter what comes against us, we are assured that you are always there for us. We thank you that although men fail us, we do not have to withdraw to a life of loneliness and that you have great plans for us.

Lord, I ask that you lead and guide me by your Holy Spirit into all truth. Show me the areas in my life where I do not trust you and teach me that I can.

Father, as I look over my life, I can see that you have never failed me. Whether it was in sickness, loss of finances, loss of friends, or even family members and loved ones that, you are always here with me.

I know that those I loved have gone before me and are with you because your Word says to be absent from this body is to be present with you. So, I trust you in every area of my life. Amen!

One more thing about trust, and that is forgiveness. The Bible tells us to "*forgive so that we may be forgiven.*" (Matthew 6:14-15) Forgiveness will allow you to feel a sense of freedom that can't be obtained any other way. It removes the burden from you to try to pay someone back. And it releases them from the burden of trying to live up to the expectations of others. It then gives God the open door to help them if they want it. Because our whole desire in life is that men come into the knowledge of who God is. We should desire that none would perish but come unto repentance. (2 Peter 3:9) Just think about how great this world could be if we all repented for our sins towards each other.

We are to pray for each other, even those who misused us. Prayer is how our trust in mankind will be restored. Firstly, we leave our good fortune up to God, and secondly, we leave vengeance up to God as well. Only He can change the hearts of men. I believe, therefore, that is why He tells us to guard our hearts. If we give all to God, we are guarding our hearts. We are protecting how we feel towards others. People will still be people; they will still lash out at you. They will still disappoint you, but trust and believe God is on your side. Trust Him, and He will direct your path.

Chapter 4 Guard your Heart

Proverbs 4:23 Guard your heart above all else, for it is the source of life. (CSB).

I know He likes me! But I just wanted to be with him all the time. He was so kind and loving. I could call him for anything, and he would come over as soon as possible to help. I was so excited to have someone I could count on. Surely, he is the one for me. I can't wait to be with him forever, is what was on my mind. You see, as a Christian woman, no matter what I may be currently experiencing, deep down inside, I expect to get married. Anytime a Christian woman is in a relationship. Most women also have that expectation, in the end, is marriage. Because God created us that way, and it is the Godly way.

How can we guard our hearts? The best way is Matthew 6:33; seek ye first the kingdom of God and His Righteousness, and all these things shall be added unto you. Reading the entire chapter of Matthew 6 will teach you so much about life. It teaches you how to give, how to pray, and most of all, it teaches you how to inquire of God. That is what this verse 33 is about. The verses that proceed 33 explain that we should not worry about anything because God will provide. This scripture is so profound because it says the birds don't plant, they don't toil, but they are fed, and they are adorned more beautifully than any garment we can make.

So, we are not supposed to enter any type of relationship without first seeking God. He is our father, and we can go to Him about everything. As a teen, my dad would tell me what was on a boy's mind, and he told me what was on mine as well. Dad didn't give me advice often, but he did tell me not to be oversexed. (Hmph, I thought, it's your fault that I am.) Dad didn't mean that I was engaging in the act. He meant there is more to a relationship than what those boys wanted from me.

Compliments are superficial; just because a guy likes you doesn't mean he has your back. Do you know that we need to have people who can pray for us? What happens if you get deathly ill or just need a financial miracle. No man can meet your every need. But if man is connected to the giver of everything (God our Father), he will be assured that the Lord will provide. He will not be concerned about how. Because man was created by God to be the head, the Lord will do it through him. And the man will be happy to let God's will be done in the lives of both of you. God will us the man as the avenue to make a way. If he is a Godly man, it will happen through prayer and supplication, as he seeks the Kingdom of God first.I heard someone say, "Everyone can be beautiful." So just because he finds you attractive, intelligent, or sweet, and just because he likes you, what else does he have to offer.

After I gave that man my whole heart and told him I wanted to get married, he asked me what else do you have to offer? And it was the second time I allowed him to come into my life, and I was like, huh? I am giving you me. That statement put things in perspective for me. But, he still needed to know what else I was bringing to the table. How could I help support his cause, and vice versa? Knowing what each of us brings to the table is the same way we need to explore relationships, whether platonic or love endeavors. What else do you bring to the table beside you, like me?

Does he want children, does he have children, and does he support them if he does? Because if he doesn't support his own children, will he be able to help you with yours. I remember one day getting on the city bus (remember I told you at the beginning of the book I don't drive.). This much younger man moved over and patted his seat for me to sit down next to him. He was so excited, and I thought, oh, what a nice young man. And then he hit on me. I was like, what (huh)? I am old enough to be your grandmother. I told him I have a lot of kids and grandchildren. He said I got money. He may or may not, but I knew that this young boy could not do anything for me.

Just like that young boy could not do anything for me, guess what outside of God no man can. So we must go to our father, knowing that without Him, we will fail. Look at every situation and sum it all up as this, that without Gods' stamp of approval, I will not move forward. We should do this in every situation. Nothing is too small to ask God about. That is what God means by seeking Him first.

Jude 24-25; *Now unto him that can keep you from falling, and to present you faultless before the presence of his glory with exceeding joy, To the only wise God our Savior, be glory and majesty, dominion and power, both now and ever. Amen.*

This scripture says that God can keep you from falling. God can make sure that everything we do is successful. All we must do is ask and listen to the answer. He will not let you mess up. He is not waiting for you to fail. So, to keep your issues limited, guard your heart by seeking the face of God. I tell you the truth, as I began writing this book for the third time, it started entirely different than my previous times. I was like, "Oh! Okay, that person, right?" So, I prayed to see if this was what He wanted me to say. Because although it is good to tell your story, we need to know what is the part that God wants us to share. There are so many dynamics to everyone's life, but there are specifics that God wants us to use to help others. Let me tell you, as a 63-year-old woman with three adult children and seven grandchildren, no husband ever, I can tell you a lot about "He Likes You."

My story is great because of God's grace. But His story is better. And the end of yours can be as well. So, guard your heart by opening it up to Jesus. Let Him come in and show you the way. Our time on earth is so short. Even if we lived to be a thousand years, there would still be something else we could do. So, please make sure that you connect with the right people and that you do things God's way.

Chapter 5 - He Likes Me Now What?

I call the story of my daughter and son-in-law's meeting one of a modern-day Cinderella. Not that he is a prince, or she is a princess, but it is a story of how God brought two people together. You see, my daughter had received what I call almost a full scholarship ride to the University of Arizona in Tucson. I was so excited because I could help her with her tuition, if I needed to. She was only lacking $1000 per year. Surely we could pay that amount. She seemed to do well while she was there. She met some good people, got the right kind of grades, and settled in nicely. However, before the year was over, she told me she believed God wanted her to go to another school. So she enrolled into GCU (Grand Canyon University), a private school where her tuition doubled immediately! Her older sister had gone to school before her, and I wasn't able to help her at all financially, and neither could her father. He died her first year from a drug overdose and some tricky play. We never found out how he ended up in the back seat of his own car.

I truly wanted to help this next child go to school. I wanted to feel like I was doing my part. However, I took it to the Lord in prayer. I was like, okay Lord, just as it has been all her life, she is in your hands. I know you will provide as you always have. And He did. She achieved both her bachelor's in communication and her master's in education. My oldest daughter, I have to give her a plug; she also has her master's in theology as well. My youngest is currently in school to become a dental assistant. As you can see, they all have ambition and gifts given by God.

Well, to make a long story short, she ended up breaking it off with the young man I thought she was going to marry. I was so surprised. They had gone through so much as friends we all thought he was the one. She went to prom with him, and they graduated from the same high school. He went out of state to college, and they broke up and got back together every time there was a break. I loved the young man, but I knew my daughter had great faith in God, and she would do as God instructed. As it so happens, she is married with three children to the man she met at GCU.

The man she married she was not interested in at first. As a matter of fact, none of us thought he was the right one for her. He seemed to be occupied with his own dreams. But, she loved him, and I believe God put that love in her. So, when you know "He Likes You;" take it to the Lord in prayer. The Bible says he that finds a wife finds a good thing and earns the favor of the Lord… (Proverbs 18:22, paraphrased.) As a Christian woman, the goal is not to date but to marry. Dating is a worldly term, and it is the world's way of doing things. God requires us to save ourselves for marriage. He only speaks of women three ways: a virgin, a married woman, and a widow. He never mentions single mothers. Not once. I know I've searched. Being a single mother and now a single grandmother, I wanted to know what benefits the Lord stored up for me. (LOL.) He does not have anything special for the single woman, other than He says that as a virgin, we are to do the work of the ministry. Don't get into condemnation because He is a restoring God, and once we turn back to Him, he welcomes us with open arms. God loves us, and remember Jesus paid it all for our sins.

You see, when you know he likes you, don't chase him; let the Lord present you to him. Then, you can let him know you are interested in him. However, leave the work to him. You are on the receiving end until marriage. Then you give yourself to him, and you take care of him. Because you are his good thing, and he is your representation of how Jesus loves the church.

In the body of Christ, we talk a lot about finding our Boaz (strength.) However, Ruth was not in love with him, and he was the one chosen for her by God. She was obedient to the mother God placed in her life. He very well may have been the most handsome man she had ever seen or even the wealthiest. Their marriage was a marriage of purpose. The same will be for you. God created you for his purpose, and everyone that is added to you is added for that reason.

One of my favorite stories in the Bible is about Isaac and Rebekah. I love this story because Abraham sent his servant to get a wife for his son. His servant prayed for the right one, and the Lord answered his prayer. Well, let's pray that the Lord will send you to the right man. I am also going to pray this for my two single daughters.

Read the entire chapter of Genesis 24 when you have time. I have added some of the verses below on how Abraham instructed the servant and the outcome. I hope you hear my heart not as a single woman but as a mature woman who has made many mistakes in her love endeavors. You see, I did not know I was wife material when I was younger. I did not think I was worthy of being anyone's wife. I thought men were only good for one thing, and that was between the hours of 11 pm and 6 am. Until I gave my life to Christ, I was unaware I was anyone's good thing.

I don't have to have men tell me I am beautiful, but it is nice to hear. We all live in the flesh. I remember getting dressed one day, and I felt uncomfortable because I can't wear metal on my upper body. No earrings or necklaces. As I was getting dressed, I heard the Lord say my neck was beautiful. I was like, wow, thank you, Lord. And another time, I went to a woman's luncheon, and the speaker gave me a Word, and the Lord said didn't I tell you once you were beautiful.

The Lord told me that Women are the Flowers of the World! So, I wrote a book with that title. He told me that there would be no beauty without women in this world. He created us so tenderly. We are the most beautiful delicate part of creation. So, when you find "He Likes You," you owe it to yourself to find out if he is the one God chose for you.

Genesis 24 *Abraham was now a very old man, and God blessed him in every way.* **2** *One day Abraham said to his household administrator, who was his oldest servant,*

3 *"Swear by Jehovah, the God of heaven and earth, that you will not let my son marry one of these local girls, these Canaanites.*

4 *Go instead to my homeland, to my relatives, and find a wife for him there."*

12 *"O Jehovah, the God of my master," he*
prayed, "show kindness to my master Abraham
and help me to accomplish the purpose of my
journey. 13 *See, here I am, standing beside this*
spring, and the girls of the village are coming
out to draw water. 14 *This is my request: When I*
ask one of them for a drink, and she says, 'Yes,
certainly, and I will water your camels too!'—let
her be the one you have appointed as Isaac's
wife. That is how I will know."

*15-16 As he was still speaking to the Lord about
this, a beautiful young girl[b] named Rebekah
arrived with a water jug on her shoulder and
filled it at the spring. (Her father was Bethuel,
the son of Nahor*, and his wife, Milcah.)
17 Running over to her, the servant asked her for
a drink.*

*18 "Certainly, sir," she said and quickly lowered
the jug for him to drink. 19 Then she said, "I'll
draw water for your camels, too, until they have
enough!"*

*50 Then Laban and Bethuel replied, "The Lord
has obviously brought you here, so what can we
say? 51 Take her and go! Yes, let her be the
wife of your master's son, as Jehovah has
directed."*

Father, in the name of Jesus, I thank you for my sister that is reading this book. Holy Spirit, reveal to her who she is in you. Let her know that now that she has been presented to the right man, to hold on to your hand and never to let it go. Let her realize that you brought them together. And since you have, that he is worth working for. Let her work through all her insecurities. I ask that you make her whole. Help her to keep her eyes on you and off of her circumstances. You are a great God, and you have great things in store for her.

Amen!

Chapter 6 You Were Created as a Helper!

Genesis 2:18; And the LORD God said, It is not good that the man should be alone; I will make him a help meet for him. (KJV)

After Adam finished naming all the animals in the Garden, the Lord put him to sleep. He then took one of the man's ribs and formed the woman. When the Lord presented the woman to Adam, Adam then named her. He called her woman because she came from him, and he named her Eve because she would be the mother of all living. The Lord created Eve to help Adam. He also created her because there was no one like him. God created every animal to produce after his own kind. Thus he created us for the same reason.

The Lord put in the woman intricate details that he did not include with the man. We have been given the gift of birth. We can not only produce mankind, but we can also feed them with our bodies. We have been given the ability to be natural nurturers, but only if we choose to do so. We are not necessarily more emotional than our male counterparts, but we are more comfortable displaying our emotions. We cry easier, and we get angry easier. We are considered more beautiful and softer as well. We are also created to submit easier.

Most women who do not know how to submit to their husbands, as the Bible says, seem to come off hard. I think it's because it's not how we were created. The Bible tells us to submit to our husbands. (Yes, and it also tells our husbands to submit to us as well.) But this book is for women, so that is why I am speaking on the woman's role. So, after you know for sure because God has confirmed that he is the one for you, now it's time to really start praying for him because he will need to get to know you. The real you. Not the one he saw that caught his eye. No, the human part about you.

He will also need to know the spiritual aspect of you. What you believe and who you believe in. We are all at different levels in our Faith, and he will need to be able to pinpoint where your Faith is. You will also need to pray for him for the same reasons. Even though you both believe in God, do you both trust God to do all that He says He will in His Word?

I remember that when I first entered my last ungodly relationship, it had been 17 years since I had been with a man. He would hurt my feelings with the way he talked to me. He seemed to be so uncaring towards me at first. His words were so hard. And then it hit me one Sunday when our Bishop was preaching. I was like, oh my, I am only used to having conversations with women who speak softly. He is not intentionally hurting my feelings. He is a man, and his way is very different from mine. Men and women do things entirely differently. Even though I was raised with four brothers, when I got older, we were separated. My brothers and my dad shared a bathroom, my mother, my sister, and I shared our own bathroom. So, we only came together for things like eating and watching TV. We had our separate chores, and until I got with him the second time around, like 30 years after I met him the first time, I was not used to men. I mention this to you because you will need to get to know him before you marry. Take your time, and don't rush into it. Enjoy the courting stage. Remember, dating is for the world. You two are together with the intention of getting married.

Also, just because you were created as a helper doesn't negate that God created you to be helped and lead at times. Don't get caught up thinking God did not call you. He did call you; you must know what that calling is and be sure that he also knows what your calling is. There was another great woman in the Bible, and she was a Prophet, a Judge, and a wife. Her name was Deborah her husband's name was Lappidoth, which means torches and can be translated as illumination. This verse, I believe, is imperative so that you can see from a biblical perspective that it is more than okay for a woman to lead a nation. Not just a woman but a man's wife who stands behind her or with her would probably be a better way of putting it.

Judges 4:4; Israel's leader at that time, the one who was responsible for bringing the people back to God, was Deborah, a prophetess, the wife of Lappidoth.

There is one more point I want to make. And this is more of a statement for husbands. God made the woman help, so wouldn't it be wise for you to hear her out when she gives you her opinion. Women were given intuition intentionally from God. There are things that He will tell her that He does not tell you. I hear so many women say that their husbands don't value their opinion. If two opinions were not necessary, then why would God give you a helper. He would have just given you a servant if a second voice was not needed.

Boundaries are protection for stepping out of the will of God. Therefore, when you find out, he has established boundaries, pay attention to them. Don't mess up your courting time by going to bed with him prematurely. And if you have already, allow God to restore the two of you. Allow Him to prepare you two for marriage. Seek the Lord regarding every aspect of your husband to be's heart. Seek older women who can teach you how to love your husband. It is biblical read Titus Chapter 2. Also, keep doing the Lords' work until you are married. Seek the Lord on how to treat him because he will be your husband, but he is not your husband yet. Respect his input, don't be so independent that he can't speak into your life. He is a Godly man and will possess Godly Wisdom. How do I know, because He is the one you prayed for, and now he is here.

Holy Spirit lead her into all truth! Teach her how to love unconditionally as you have loved us. Teach her how to be a wife, a mother, and a teacher. You told us to seek you first in everything we do, so Lord, teach her how to reach out to you. So, father, I pray these prayers for every woman who reads this book and my daughters that We will learn how to love as you have loved us!

Chapter 7 Gods Original Plan

As I reminisce on my story, I realize that God had a plan for you and me from the very beginning of time. Although, His plan includes a story of redemption. However, as stated in the book of Jude, He is able to keep us from falling. That means that if we follow His original plan, we will not need redemption.

The very first boy I was with stays with me in my heart forever. Not that I did not love others, but I know that no one else can take the place of the first. I want you to take a trip with me. This is for those of you who need redemption but also thought for those of you who have not yet taken that first plunge.

What if you had waited, gotten counseling, and found out the differences you had with that first love could have been solved? What would happen if you found out those things that irritated you were the missing pieces to what you needed to balance you? The Bible says iron sharpens iron. Whenever you scrape iron against iron, there is friction. Neither of the pieces will sharpen; it will remain dull without friction.

It is difficult for me to articulate these words. The reason is that my first was so abusive. He became my first child's father and then my pimp. How did that all happen? Drugs! He became so insecure that he would get angry at me for being with other men. Still, before I had sex with him, he was a totally different person. He seemed to respect me. I wish I had gotten to know more about him before being with him. He had a lot of family issues.

A few years ago, I spoke to his sister, and I found out he was neglected as a child. During my interactions with him, I found he was bitter and starved for his father's love. I got to see firsthand how he was so very jealous of his gay and only brother. As a child, he didn't get what he needed to thrive. As a young man, He didn't do well in school, but he tried to find love. He was with many females, trying to find the love he lacked as a child. I couldn't fill his void, but God could have.

I also found out that people thought he had it made and was just acting out. As a very young child, some people that I grew up with knew their father had a great job, so they thought he had everything he needed and just wanted to hang out with the tough guys when he didn't need to. They thought he should have been at home reaping the benefits that his dad provided. So it is true that you never know what goes on behind closed doors.

I think the reason we got involved with prostitution although I thought I could do it and then pay my way through school. (Which the GI Bill would have paid for me.) It was so he could prove, to his friends, he could do just as well with hustling as they did. I wasn't ever very good at it. I was too honest, and the Lord had a different plan for my life.

After I finally settled down my last two years of school, I again began to get good grades. I even did some of the senior boys' math work as a Junior for them so they could graduate. Unfortunately, I decided to settle into school just a little too late and ended up taking and passing the GED, the same month I should have graduated. I could have gone to college or gotten a job as my sister did. Instead, I got so got up with him, and I lost myself. You know, it was because he touched me the way I liked it. Not only did he need Jesus, so did I.

He has been coming to me in my dreams as a permanent presence in my life from the time I gave my life to the Lord in my 30's. I do not know if he was God's original intent for me or not. I just wanted to visit this with you because if He wasn't God's original intent for me, then I should not have been with him. We are bringing children into the world willy-nilly, making it hard for them to have a good start. When all we have to do is acknowledge the father in everything, we do.

Children need both a male and female presence in their lives to live a balanced life. That is the way God created us. And I believe He wanted us all to live together as a family. In Genesis, Adam declared that Eve is bone of his bone and that a man should leave his family to cleave to his wife. Gods' original intent was for a man and woman to live together and raise their children with the nurture and admonition of the Lord.

My family was very dysfunctional, and although I grew up with four brothers and an athletic sister, I knew how to act like a lady. My father felt there were specific roles that females played in the home. At first, I did not think it was fair. Nonetheless, I was taught how to dress a certain way. I was only allowed to show so much skin as a young teen. I learned how to clean the house and myself. These were things my mother told me to do. However, my father insisted I do them.

Even though he was not very nice to my brothers, he felt there were chores men should do. He knew how to cook and clean the kitchen. I don't ever recall having to clean up after he cooked, other than the dishes as usual. My mother could dig up a yard, paint a living room, and cook like nobody's business, and my brothers could do the same. Having a male and female presence teaches boys how to be men and girls how to be ladies. Learning is caught more than it is taught.

Chapter 8 New Beginnings

Isaiah 48:6; "You have heard; now see all this, and will you not declare it?

From this time forth, I announce to you new things. Hidden things that you have not known. (ESB)

With any Word of God, we have the opportunity to start over. God never holds us back because of past mistakes we have made. God is a loving and kind Father. He loves us so much that He will always give us the opportunity to correct any mistakes that we have made. The whole story of Jesus is that Jesus came into the world to redeem us from the repercussions caused in the Garden. I wanted to say the sins that Adam did, but because of the blood of Jesus, it doesn't matter who sinned because He has now paid the price for all sins. We have been made new. The Word says if you are in Christ Jesus, then you are a new creature, and all old things have passed away. (2 Corinthians 5:17)

In Isaiah, the Lord is letting us know He has new things for us, and that if we will declare it, which means if we will say what He says and believe in our heart what He has spoken to you through this book what He has said will come to pass. You see, the Word of God is so perfect that no matter who reads it or hears it, whatever they need is provided. Some of you are reading this book because you are looking for a mate. While others, like myself, have had many and now want to rest in whatever God has for them.

That is why I wanted to write this book so that you would know that just because someone says you are beautiful and he is a good guy does not mean he is the guy for you. The Lord has new things in store for you. You are not stuck. You can move forward and become everything that He speaks into your ears. My most favorite thing to do is to let young men and young women know that you do not have to participate in the things of the world to have riches. The Bible does say that money is the answer to everything. (Ecclesiastes 10:19)

Additionally, it states that wisdom is the principal thing. (Proverbs 4:7) Without wisdom, money is fleeting. Even if you have enough to do everything you want, without doing things Gods' way, in the end, you will perish. Meaning you will be unhappy and unfulfilled. I know some of this is repetitive, and it's because I want you to operate for the purpose that God planned for you. Outside of God's desire for you, you will not have peace. In the past few years, we have seen so many celebrities go to jail for misconduct. Not to get money, but because they had money. And really, isn't that what we are chasing. Oh, I know some of you will say I just want love, and I know he's not the best for me, but "He likes me, he really does."

Well, God has the best life for you. Even if you think you only have two pennies to rub together, He will see to it that all your needs are met. King David said I have never seen the righteous forsaken or his seed begging bread. If you are in Christ Jesus, there is no way your needs will go unmet. You just have to do it His way. Doing it His way, you can sleep well at night, what else could you possibly need.

I will leave you with two more points, "What does it profit a man to gain the whole world and lose his soul?" (Luke 9:25) I mean, God promises us wealth and riches can be in our house (Psalms 112:3). All we have to do is follow His plan. Every day He sets before us life and death. Every day He gives us the opportunity to do it His way.

Did you know God loves all His children the same, and He will provide for all His children the same according to their faith? Whatever you can believe Him for is what you can have. If you delight yourself in the Lord, He will give you the desires of your heart. (Psalms 37:4) Now, you will have to work to keep it, and the enemy will not be happy sitting back watching you prosper. So, although the Lord adds no sorrows to His blessings, the enemy will try to get it from you. Even in the relationship that God purposes for, your disagreements may come, and even the desire to give up may come, but when God gives you the right one, stick with him. He will be worth it. Every couple that has been together for years has had to overcome many things; now they know each other and can rest assured they are with the right person. They can see it was the Lords' doing.

Again, Let's pray

I pray Gods' manifold blessing over you, Father, in the name of Jesus. I just ask that you open our eyes so that we can see you. Lord, that we will not be impressed by anything that is not from you. I pray that we have the gift of discernment (1Corinthians 12:10) so that we will know you when you show up and that we will know any spirit that is not from you when it shows up. Father teach us to judge rightfully. Father, we thank you for your love towards us. That, you are doing new things in our lives. We just have to say what you say and operate in the faith that you have so freely given each of us. Lord, we have ears to hear your Word and eyes to see everything that you say!

Lord, we stand on Your Word!

James 2:14 Tells us Faith without works is dead. All we have to do is believe what you say and walk it out.

Conclusion:

The hardest thing I deal with daily is being out of alignment with God when I conceived my children. In the book of Psalm 127:3 Verse, It says: Lo, children are a heritage of the LORD: and the fruit of the womb is his reward. (KJV). So, think about your future children before you think the fact that "He Likes You" is enough for you. Is it enough for your children? Because it is inevitable if you are fertile to conceive. And is he the man you want to raise children with? Once you conceive, then he is a part of your life forever. Even if he is a dead-beat dad and never comes around, you will still carry him with you wherever you go.

Remember, the children are a heritage. Children are your possession and your reward from the Lord. You are responsible for children. Their outcome will be your reward. So I do want to say no matter the circumstance if you have the opportunity to raise children, seek the Lord because it is never easy. Satan comes to steal, kill and destroy every good thing the Lord has given you. Jesus came, however, so that you will have a good life.

If you have had children out of alignment with the Word of God, just know they are your reward. And God is on their side as well. He will take care of them.

My oldest daughter was born three months before I turned 19. She was prematurely born at a little over seven months. I thought because I was of age, it was okay for me to have sex. (Druggies think differently than normal society.) As a young girl, I got a late start with puberty. When I initially started my menstruation, I bled twice a month. The doctor put me on birth control pills to regulate me. I took birth control pills for four years, so the doctor told me I should rest my body for a while. He assured me that I probably would not get pregnant because I had taken them so long, and they were so potent. She was the prettiest little 3 pounds, 14-ounce curly-headed baby I had ever seen. I knew absolutely nothing about taking care of a baby. Thank the Lord for my family. Reverend Felecia O'Neal made it with the Lord looking out for her as she helped to raise her younger sisters.

Although I had a miscarriage shortly after my first baby girl was born, I got pregnant again, without a husband seven years later. Seven years after she was born, I discovered that the man I thought was her father wasn't. I thought she looked like him, same hands, but it apparently was not so. And the man who is her father, I cut it off with him before I knew I was pregnant. She was so athletic and rambunctious, and beautiful as well. My last baby girl was born in my mid-thirties. She was so beautiful. Big eyes that followed me everywhere I went. I loved her to pieces, my last child. You see, the year before, I had lost another baby. I found out one night in the ER I was pregnant. The next day, the baby was gone. So her dad was like, that's okay, we can try again. And we did, and we fought over her because I found out in the middle of my pregnancy that he already had a girlfriend. I have no idea where she was on the weekends when we spent the night, but there she was right in the middle of my pregnancy.

I am telling you these stories because God can restore you, but even better than that, God can keep you from falling. So, seek the Lord before getting involved with any man and let Him establish your relationships.

No matter what we have done; The Bible tells us we are ...fearfully and wonderfully made (Psalms 139:14).

I love the Lord, and I am so excited about what He is going to do in your life. He wants you to know how important you are to Him and That He has hand-selected someone just for you. You are more beautiful than you can ever imagine, you are the apple of His eye, and He wants you to know that.

Lord, for those who desire a husband, I thank you that their faith fails not, and Lord, those that desire to remain single, I pray that their faith fails not.

Most of all, I pray that you will be number one all of their lives.

About The Author

Annette O'Neal is a mother of three beautiful daughters, grandmother to seven beautiful grandchildren.

She is an ordained minister and advocate for all who seek freedom from the trauma which has caused them pain. Whether it was from past hurts of self-infliction, or forcefully placed on them. Her one desire is that all would come into the knowledge of the Lord Jesus Christ who has already paid the price for their freedom.

www.ingramcontent.com/pod-product-compliance
Lightning Source LLC
LaVergne TN
LVHW051707080426
835511LV00017B/2780

* 9 7 8 0 5 7 8 2 8 2 7 9 4 *